Cenzoo
The story of a baby gorilla

Joe Verrengia

in cooperation with
the Denver Zoo

D1736597

Cenzoo

The story of a baby gorilla

Joe Verrengia

in cooperation with the Denver Zoo

International Standard Book Number 1-57098-128-0

Library of Congress Card Catalog Number 96-72309

Published by Roberts Rinehart Publishers
5455 Spine Road
Boulder, Colorado 80301
Tel 303.530.4400
Fax 303.530.4488

Distributed to the trade by Publishers Group West

Published in the UK and Ireland by
Roberts Rinehart Publishers
Trinity House, Charleston Road
Dublin 6, Ireland
10 9 8 7 6 5 4 3 2 1

Editor: Alice Levine

Contents

Jeremy Baer-Simon

Much of Jo-Ray-K's day is spent relaxing while Cenzoo plays.

Preface

The warm and very insistent bundle of black fur—a baby gorilla—that nestled in the crook of my arm represented everything that is right and wrong about the lives of gorillas today.

I had traveled to the tiny central African nation of Rwanda to accompany two primatologists who were following the lead of Dian Fossey and George Schaller in protecting and studying the very rare mountain gorilla. Our trip in 1993 occurred during a cease-fire in the civil war between the Hutu government and insurgent Tutsi rebels. Less than a year later, in 1994, clashes within the gorillas' jungle park escalated into full-scale war and widespread massacres that claimed a half-million lives and transformed another 2 million people into refugees.

During that lull, the three of us were to travel deep into the forests of the towering Virunga mountain range to see whether the apes had survived and to visit Fossey's historic and remote research camp. But the airlines had lost my luggage somewhere between Denver and Kigali, the Rwandan capital. Our travel permits into the war zone and the national park where the gorillas live were ensnared by bureaucratic red tape. As one day in dusty Kigali dragged into the next, I used the delay to scrounge outdoor gear from American and European aid workers who had elected to remain in the country despite the dangers and mounting food shortages.

It was in the backyard garden of a Belgian conservationist that I met the little gorilla. He was not a mountain gorilla—a species

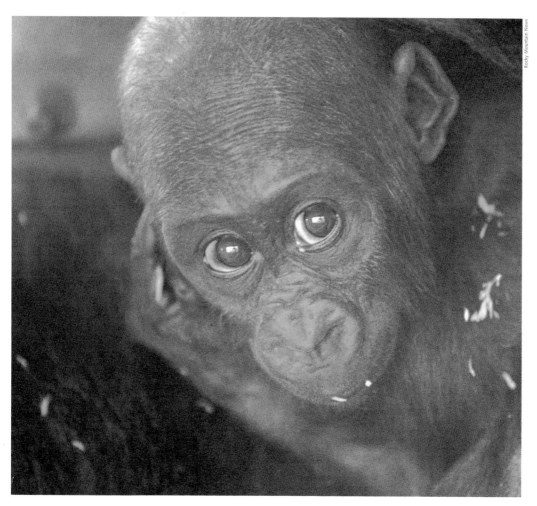

Cenzoo often snuggles in the comfort and security
of his mother's embrace.

once vilified in its native land that had recently become such a lucrative source of tourist dollars that the desperately poor country issued a stamp in its honor and engraved its likeness on its new currency. This 18-month-old toddler was believed to be an eastern lowland gorilla who might have come from the jungles of neighboring Zaire. Customs officers at the airport in Kigali had discovered him near death in a crate that had been transported under Egyptian diplomatic immunity.

If he had reached his destination undetected, he would probably have fetched upward of $50,000 on the black market that trades in exotic and endangered pets. That is a large sum anywhere, but it is a king's ransom in central Africa, where the average income in many nations hovers at $250 a year. A Western zoo would not have purchased the gorilla, but many countries in Asia and the Middle East are lax about animal collections and unconcerned about endangered species. The gorilla would probably have died

in the private menagerie of a wealthy family if conservationists had not stepped in after he was discovered in the crate and had not nursed him back to health.

By the time I strolled into the conservationist's backyard, the gorilla weighed at least 30 pounds. His coat was coal-black and coarse. He approached me directly across the lawn, motioning with a crooked hand as if to say, "C'mon, c'mon." Then he grabbed my leg as if it were a rope and hoisted his way into my arms. I tried resting his warm body on my hip and hugged him to my side. He was about the size of a puppy. But puppies are like soft, wriggling sacks and this baby gorilla already had steely muscles beneath his dense coat. He was not helpless; his grip was strong and sure. Standing in the midday heat, I soon felt his weight. But he was not going to get down until he was ready. His grip, and my hug, became tighter as I walked him around the garden. His eyes were amber gold. He had tiny gray fingers tipped with tinier nails. His nose was flat and his skin was black and wrinkled. In some ways he looked like a very old, wizened man. I could not imagine him as an adult—a silverback with a domed head larger than a football helmet. Fully grown, he would weigh as much as three men and possess the strength of 10 or 20.

Eventually, he tipped upside down and loosened his grip. As I relaxed my hug, he readily climbed down my leg head-first. A moment later, I spied him across the garden vigorously bending the pliable trunk of an ornamental tree. It was an unforgettable encounter. He came to me freely and departed contentedly. That brief stroll left me with an appreciation for primates that no interview, book, or television documentary could provide.

But our brief meeting occurred because poachers had ripped the young gorilla from his mother's grasp in his native forest hundreds of miles away. They had certainly killed her and probably others trying to protect him. And although conservationists had rescued him from that stifling crate and were treating him generously, the house and garden were but a comfortable prison. He soon would be too strong and agile to live with even the most sympathetic human family. And it would never be possible to return him to the wild— even if he could find his social group. Given the trauma he suffered, his exposure to humans, and the natural lessons and socialization he missed, it is certain that he would have starved or been killed in what had been his natural habitat.

Within months after our meeting, he had been relocated to a primate sanctuary in neighboring Burundi that was operated by the Jane Goodall Foundation. There he thrived, even though he was a gorilla among chimps. But he could not remain there forever and conservationists from Colorado to Nairobi debated his fate. By that time, ethnic hatred had consumed Rwanda and was spilling into Burundi. Conservation programs were reduced to rubble and Western aid workers fled for

Cenzoo sometimes struggles when his mother tries to groom him.

Cenzoo: The story of a baby gorilla

their lives. Wild mountain gorillas vanished into the deepest recesses of the forest as national park guards scattered into refugee camps. It was not until early 1997 that the programs were beginning to recover, but the peace was far from secure.

I lost track of my captive gorilla friend in the welter of events and headlines. Then came Cenzoo.

When I saw his Chicago zookeeper carry Cenzoo off an airplane to begin a new life in Denver, the memory of that day in the Kigali garden clubbed me in the head and I could not help but feel helpless and angry. Captivity is no substitute for nature. But the future for Cenzoo and other gorillas in zoos is secure and predictable. Captive gorillas typically live more than 35 years with the benefits of a scientifically balanced diet, regular veterinary care, and, increasingly, generously proportioned, natural-style enclosures. Although the zoo habitat cannot duplicate life in the wild, curators believe the animals' lives are more enriched today, especially when compared to zoos that were built like maximum-security locker rooms with steel bars and tile walls. Research conducted in zoos adds to our knowledge about gorilla genetics and behavior and may prove useful in the extensive effort to preserve and protect species in the wild.

Cenzoo's life in the Denver zoo offers a stark contrast to native gorilla

Alert and secure in his mother's embrace, Cenzoo keeps a curious watch on the events around him.

populations in struggling African nations like Rwanda that are beset by war, hunger, poaching, and burgeoning human populations. Because gorillas are the most popular attraction in zoos, Cenzoo may be something more than a curiosity. As he matures, he may offer visitors memorable lessons about the dignity and power of these close primate cousins and provide curators and conservationists with the kind of information and revenues they have long needed to effectively protect great apes in the wild.

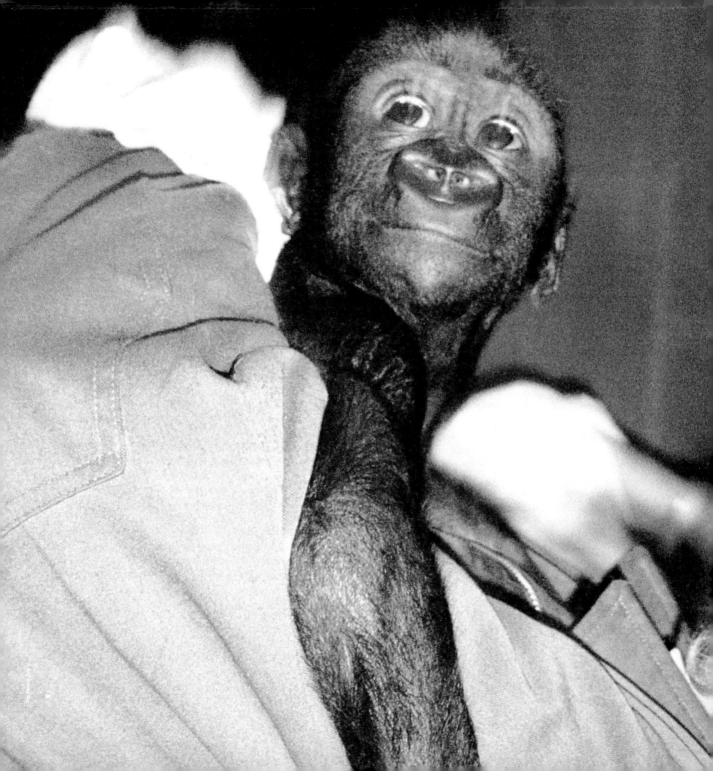

Chapter 1
Cenzoo arrives in Denver

United Airlines flight 237 from Chicago on April 23, 1996, was, in many ways, a smooth and uneventful ride. As the plane approached Denver International Airport, lingering winter storms were confined to the Rocky Mountains 100 miles west. Midafternoon temperatures in Denver zoomed to 70 degrees under clear prairie skies.

To the passengers' satisfaction, the crowded Boeing 767 pulled up to Concourse B on time. Two hundred people jumped from their seats when an announcement from the pilot froze them in mid-scuffle. "This is the captain speaking. We have a special passenger in first class this afternoon who needs to disembark the aircraft as soon as we reach the gate. Please be patient for a few minutes until he is on his way." People craned their necks to catch a glimpse of the celebrity. Those who looked out of the windows to the tarmac were amazed to see airport employees, security vehicles, and television cameras surrounding the plane. Inside the airport, travelers pressed against the large concourse windows and stared at the unusual scene.

Cenzoo's boarding pass, marked "Baby Gorilla," on United Airlines flight 237.

Ramp workers secured the jetway against the aircraft's front door. At the bottom of the steel emergency stairs, a dozen flight attendants lined up, smiling and waving, to form a welcoming committee. Who was important enough to deserve such VIP treatment? A rock star? A presidential candidate?

A baby gorilla. A baby western lowland gorilla, to be precise.

Cenzoo never appeared frightened or intimidated by the activity around him during his transfer to Denver.

Cenzoo rides in Eric Meyer's lap in the first-class section of United Airlines flight 237 from Chicago to Denver.

Lincoln Park Zoo

In the first class cabin, 10-week old Cenzoo sat in the lap of his zookeeper, Eric Meyer. He twirled Meyer's long, curly black hair around his tiny, wrinkled fingers. Occasionally, his bald head appeared over Meyer's shoulder as he cautiously investigated the commotion.

Below, in the airplane's pressurized, heated cargo hold, Cenzoo's father, mother, and aunt were in their reinforced travel crates. For all four, the journey had started before dawn at the Lincoln Park Zoo in Chicago, Cenzoo's birthplace. Before the day's end, they would arrive at their new, larger home in Primate Panorama at Denver Zoological Gardens. Together, they would form the core of the zoo's expanded captive breeding program for endangered primates.

Although airlines often transport animals—including wild and rare species, flying certainly is not natural for a gorilla. But it is the swiftest and most controlled method of transporting animals long distances. Officials at the Denver and Chicago zoos agreed flying was safer than shipping the apes by truck for two days on interstate highways during the early spring.

But air travel is not without risks to the animals. Delays can lead to stress and dehydration if the animals spend too many hours in cramped crates and noisy industrial cargo facilities. Safety is another concern; an animal may act unpredictably when crated in an unfamiliar environment, or it may become disturbed by the vibrations and strange sensations of flying. Tranquilizers help, but veterinarians are reluctant to heavily sedate animals whose sensitive nervous systems may not tolerate the medications. Diseases are yet another risk. Great apes are susceptible to the same infections as humans, especially to illnesses that are commonly spread in airplanes—like colds and flu. But unlike humans, the apes' immune systems do not have adequate defenses.

Although zoo curators worried that 10-week-old Cenzoo and his mother might become distraught over being separated during the long and unsettling trip, the potential for injury to the 8-pound infant was enormous if he traveled by truck and airplane in the same crate as his mother for 12 hours or more.

Zoo officials pondered their options as pressure to transfer the apes mounted. Their enclosure in Chicago was crowded with a dozen other gorillas and the new ape house in Denver was ready. The gorillas would need several weeks to become accustomed to their new home before it was opened to the public in July. Finally, the zoos and United

Airlines reached an unorthodox compromise. Cenzoo would ride in Meyer's arms as a passenger, where he would be more comfortable and safer. And, they would ride in first class, where Cenzoo would have less

Ramp workers secure steel crate carrying an adult gorilla.

Eric Meyer of Lincoln Park Zoo carries Cenzoo from the airplane at Denver International Airport.

contact with humans then he would in economy class. His mother, father, and aunt would ride in the cargo hold.

Settling into the plane's wide leather chair was a first for both the infant gorilla and his human chaperone. The event was unusual for the United flight crew, too. Senior flight attendant Shirley Hoff, 49, made sure that Cenzoo and Meyer received all the perks that the other six passengers in first class enjoyed. Hoff, a flight attendant for 26 years, noted that Cenzoo—her first ape passenger—did not behave much differently from a human baby flying in a parent's lap. If anything, Cenzoo was better behaved than most infants. He nursed contentedly on a bottle of water and played with toys during the 2-hour flight. Meyer rocked him while he napped. The only time Cenzoo fussed was when the plane descended and the air pressure in the cabin changed. "He sounded like a bird squawking," Hoff said.

When the plane landed in Denver, Meyer wrapped Cenzoo in a striped towel and a United Airlines T-shirt. The hardest part of the trip was still to come. He took a deep breath, gathered Cenzoo in his arms, and ducked down the jetway's metal staircase. Cheers and applause greeted them like a great gust of wind. He could see the grinning faces of hundreds of people—flight attendants, baggage handlers, mechanics, and custodians. Many of them were waving bananas. A posse of reporters and photographers surged closer to the stairs, pointing video cameras and telephoto lenses. Meyer instinctively hugged Cenzoo a little tighter as he carefully walked down the stairs.

But the unruly scene did not scare Cenzoo; it fascinated him. He grabbed Meyer's shirt and pulled himself upright to get a better view. His amber-brown eyes were wide and bright, and his coal-black bald head appeared huge as it bobbed atop his narrow shoulders. Sensing his tiny companion's curiosity, Meyer paused at the bottom of the stairs and briefly posed with Cenzoo. Strobe lights flashed. Motor drives

Flight attendants greet Cenzoo and Eric Meyer at the bottom of the jetway. More than 100 airline employees, zoo personnel, and media acknowledged the baby gorilla's arrival.

Cenzoo's ride to his new home at the Denver Zoo
started out as a media event with everyone wanting
to get close to the curious gorilla.

whirred. Cenzoo played with Meyer's hair again. He accepted another bottle of water and slurped contentedly from its nipple. Reporters shouted questions. "Did he enjoy the flight?" "Did he watch the movie?" Meyer nodded his head affirmatively when asked if Cenzoo was tolerating the journey, but he shook off the rest of the questions. His job was to get Cenzoo into the van parked a few steps from the plane. There he would be safe from the crowd and less vulnerable to sneezes and accidents.

Meyer sighed visibly when the van's door slid shut with a thunk. People pressed against the door and stared through its windows as if it were a rolling zoo exhibit. "Would you give him this?" one flight attendant shouted over the jet noise, waving a bright yellow banana. Denver Zoo mammal curator Michael Kinsey, who was standing guard by the van door, appeared shocked, then laughed. "He doesn't eat bananas," he yelled over the din.

Meanwhile, on the other side of the plane, the crates holding the adult apes were being unloaded from the cargo hold along with hundreds of suitcases, cardboard boxes, ski and golf bags. Their wood-and-steel containers, each as large as a small car, rumbled down a ramp and slid with a clatter onto flatbeds. Ramp crews secured them with tough cargo netting and used fork lifts to transfer them to a waiting truck. The gorillas included Cenzoo's father, a 573-pound silverback named Koundu, his mother, Jo-Ray-K, and a second adult female named Bassa who serves as Cenzoo's surrogate aunt. The apes had been mildly sedated in Chicago before dawn, but now they were alert. Upon landing in Denver, they startled the passengers in the cabin above them by rocking their crates and banging on the walls. They jostled their crates again when the crowd on the tarmac surrounded them. But they settled down when they were in the truck. By 4:30 P.M., Cenzoo and his family began their slow parade under police escort from the airport to the Denver Zoo.

Chapter 2
Cenzoo's new home

Darkness had enveloped the Denver Zoo by the time Cenzoo and his family moved into their new home, at Primate Panorama. Moonbeams passed through tiny windows at the top of the new three-story playroom. Cloaked in shadows and draped in netting and ropes, the climbing apparatus resembled a jungle canopy. Below, in a small, secluded chamber, a tender mother-and-child reunion was taking place. Jo-Ray-K had crafted a night nest from a great mound of yellow straw. She cuddled and nursed her infant. Soon Cenzoo closed his eyes and suckled peacefully.

Two hours earlier, the atmosphere had been anything but warm and snugly. Overhead lights glared and heavy machinery growled. Curators nervously paced the concrete passageway connecting the playroom and the sleeping chambers. Jo-Ray-K's separation from Cenzoo during the disorienting day-long trip worried them. Any separation of a mother gorilla from her offspring, even for sound reasons, is unusual and alarming. In the wild, a gorilla baby clings desperately to its mother's rough black coat as she forages for food in shrubs, low trees, and high grass. Although the infant becomes more curious and playful in adolescence, even then it rarely ventures very far on its own. Most gorilla mothers are notably attentive, but Jo-Ray-K had gained a reputation in Chicago for being comparatively casual toward her offspring. Would the

Jeremy Baer-Simon

Jo-Ray-K crafted a night nest from a great mound of yellow straw.

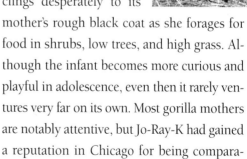

Cenzoo, age 4 1/2 months, adjusts to his new home at the Denver Zoo.

trip and the new surroundings in Denver prompt her to reject her baby, who would be carrying the scent of a human zookeeper and of others? Would the curators have to rescue Cenzoo and hand-raise him?

There was only one way to find out. With the help of a forklift, more than a dozen zoo employees maneuvered Jo-Ray-K's wood-and-steel, 700-pound crate against the sleeping chamber's sliding door. The gorilla's sharp odor quickly filled the hall. Jo-Ray-K shifted her bulk inside the crate,

The Denver Zoo

Finally at home, Koundu's crate is unloaded at Primate Panorama.

but remained silent. The crate fit snugly against the chamber's door, but zoo officials remained wary. Jo-Ray-K probably would scamper through the opening and investigate her new surroundings, grateful to stretch her long arms and compact legs. But she might try to bolt. So technicians slung wire cables around the crate and fastened them to hooks

in the concrete wall, in effect lashing the crate to the chamber's steel door frame. On a count of three, curators raised the gate to the crate and the chamber door simultaneously. As expected—but to everyone's relief—Jo barreled out of the crate and into her new digs. After a quick look around, she overturned a welcome basket of fresh vegetables and started to snack.

Then came the risky part—reintroducing Cenzoo to his mother. Zookeepers doffed his travel diaper and gently placed him in the "howdy window" of a second sleeping chamber. This window allows animals to see each other before they can make physical contact. Jo-Ray-K eyed her baby with interest. Cenzoo started whimpering. After several minutes, zookeepers decided to raise the grating separating them. They hoped the mother would scoop up her baby, but it was possible that she would ignore him or even swat him aside. And they would be helpless to stop her. Jo-Ray-K opted to avoid Cenzoo. She stared at him, but would not reach out for him no matter how much he whimpered and wailed. "It's OK, Jo. You can hold him," her Chicago zookeeper, Eric Meyer, gently encouraged.

But it was no use. An hour passed. With Meyer's concurrence, the Denver curators opted for Plan B. They pushed the crate holding Bassa, the other female gorilla, into position and lashed it to the chamber door frame. Repeating the procedure used with Jo-Ray-K, they lifted the gates simultaneously. Bassa immediately knuckle-walked into the chamber and picked up Cenzoo, who stopped whimpering and nestled against her ample belly. Soon the two females were passing the baby back and forth. By 8:00 P.M., Cenzoo was clinging to Jo-Ray-K's back. Minutes later, he burrowed beneath her arm and began to nurse.

The zookeepers were relieved and exhausted. Some walked outside, hoping the cool spring air might refresh them. Others

Cenzoo and his mother, Jo-Ray-K, rests comfortably in the straw of the indoor playroom after being reunited at Primate Panorama.

Eric Meyer carries Cenzoo down the service road behind the Denver Zoo to the back door of Primate Panorama. He is flanked, left, by Barbara Weber of the Brookfield Zoo in Chicago, and, right, Mammal Curator Mark Rosenthal of the Lincoln Park Zoo and Denver Zoo General Curator John Wortman.

Koundu, Cenzoo's farther, is always on the lookout for danger to his charges.

leaned against the thick walls of the Great Ape House and closed their eyes. "It will probably go back and forth all night," said Denver Zoo General Curator John Wortman. "But the mother picked up the baby. They've connected."

But the zookeepers' job was only half completed. It was time for Phase 2: introducing Cenzoo's father to the new exhibit. Tired zookeepers realized that their work with the females and the baby was just a warmup. Koundu, one of the largest gorillas in captivity, a 20-year-old silverback, weighed more than twice as much as Jo-Ray-K and Bassa combined, More daunting than his weight is his physique. His body-fat ratio is a rock-hard 4 percent and all that muscle is packed on a 5-foot-4-inch frame. His transit crate was bolted with so much reinforcing steel that it weighed more than 1,000 pounds, bringing the combined weight of ape and box to three-quarters of a ton. The females' crates had been moved by a forklift, but zookeepers had to lift Koundu's crate with the scoop of a front-end loader and drive it across the gorillas' outdoor exercise yard. With a great diesel roar, it chugged up a utility ramp and directly into the playroom, where it pushed the crate up against the door of the final sleeping chamber.

A half-dozen zookeepers quickly lassoed the box with much thicker steel cables that they had used for the females' crates, criss-crossing them around the back and securing them to the wall hooks. The room was cleared of all personnel except for a single man to operate the doors, and he kept one hand on the exit door behind him. Koundu had remained motionless despite the noise and jostling. It was not clear if he was woozy from the journey or gathering himself for an explosive angry charge. Although he had tolerated long trips

Koundu's crate was too large to be moved through the service door. The tractor maneuvered it across the gorillas' outside yard and through the door to the indoor playroom.

by jet before, this time he had been separated from his females and his baby. If Koundu saw an opening, he might very well burst from his crate and go on a rampage.

The gorillas' move was closed to the public, but it attracted a crowd of zoo staff and volunteers who wanted a glimpse of Primate Panorama's new stars. Curator Wortman passed a warning through the great ape house much like a miner about to detonate dynamite. When they opened the gate, Koundu charged—right into his chamber. He covered 15 feet in a single stride like a hurdler bursting out of the starting block. Then he hoisted himself onto the hammock of cargo netting that hung from the ceiling. After

Eric Meyer holds a wriggling Cenzoo behind Primate Panorama.

peering down for a few minutes, he descended cautiously and approached the metal grating that opened to the exhibit's service hallway. If anyone ventured towards him, Koundu would shake the grating or give it a tremendous whack with his massive forearm.

Several minutes passed. The females could be heard shifting nervously in the adjacent chamber. Zoo officials agreed it was time to try to calm Koundu so the gorillas and humans could get some rest after a trip that had started 16 hours earlier. Just then, Koundu stuck a huge gray hand through a slot in the grating and gestured that he wanted a treat. Eric Meyer quickly complied with a handful of golden raisins and spoke to the silverback in a low murmur. The seasoned zoo curators ,who witnessed the transformation, admired Meyer's rapport with the gorilla and gasped at Koundu's massive presence. "He is," marveled mammal curator Michael Kinsey, "one handsome guy."

Koundu, Cenzoo's 20-year-old father, a silverback, shows his expressive mug.

Chapter 3
The primate portrait

The natural biological barriers between great apes, humans, and other primates are not nearly as formidable as the thick plates of observation glass and the finely woven metal mesh that separate Cenzoo and his gorilla family from visitors. More than 225 species of primates with varying characteristics inhabit the Earth. Primates range in size from the largest—gorillas like Koundu who weigh more than 500 pounds—to the smallest—the mouse lemur that weighs 3 ounces. Humans, who number more than 5 billion, are the most abundant of primates. But several primate species are nearly extinct; there are only 620 mountain gorillas in east equatorial Africa and fewer than 200 golden lion tamarins in the Atlantic coastal rain forest of Brazil.

Regardless of their size or abundance, all primates share basic physical characteristics, which have not changed much for tens of millions of years.

- *Primates' forward-looking eyes provide overlapping fields of vision, which enable them to focus on fine detail and accurately judge depth and distance.*
- *Primates have versatile hands with flexible and sensitive fingers. The thumb is opposable, which gives it the ability to press against the fingers to pinch and to stretch out to grip large branches and rocks. The large toes of apes and monkeys are opposable as well.*
- *Primates have large brains in relation to their bodies. They are clever, are able to solve problems, and have long memories.*

Within the primate family are several orders, each of which is characterized by specific attributes. Apes, monkeys, and humans are anthropoids (higher primates), which evolved in the past 35 million years. Some examples, now extinct, developed in areas such as the American West that are far removed from the homes of apes and monkeys today. Great apes and humans both belong to the same subgroup within anthropoids known as hominoids. Gorillas, chimpanzees, and orangutans are pongidae; humans are hominids. Hominids probably split from the great apes about 7 million years ago.

Great apes are characterized by their large size, intelligence, tree-climbing ability, and the absence of a tail. They breed year-round and tend to have a single young born after an 8 1/2-month gestation. Monkeys are smaller, with tails and smaller brains. Many species live in trees, but they run, scamper and leap in the branches rather than climb. They breed year-round with a single young born after a 4- to 6-month gestation.

Humans and great apes share more than 98 percent of the same genes despite disparities in their size, temperaments and habits. Chimpanzees and humans share 98.4 percent of the same genetic material, making them our closest animal relative. Chimpanzees do not have our bucket-shaped pelvis, long leg bones, and arched feet, which are required for upright walking.

The gorilla is the second-closest human relative. Like the chimp, it walks on its knuckles and has short, sturdy legs. Despite its size and enormous power, it is more peaceful than the chimp and avoids other animals. Gorillas, which live in groups of 5 to 15, form the most stable social organizations of the great apes. The group typically consists of one dominant male, or "silverback,"

The Denver Zoo

A family of Black Howler Monkeys, distant cousins to gorillas, live in Primate Panorama at the Denver Zoo.

A silverback mountain gorilla feeds in the dense foliage of Volcanos National Park in Rwanda. An adult mountain gorilla eats up to 50 pounds of vegetation per day.

Gorilla researcher Dr. Dieter Stecklis of the Dian Fossey Gorilla Fund observes mountain gorillas napping in their day nest. He's wearing rubber gloves to protect his hands from stinging nettles.

three or four breeding females and four or five offspring of varying ages. Some groups as large as 36 animals have been observed. But very large groups are rare because a dominant male cannot easily defend or control such a large harem. Large groups split as females begin to breed with younger subordinate males to avoid inbreeding and to receive more attentive care and protection.

Males occasionally fight within their group for the right to be the dominant silverback and to breed with the females. When groups cross paths in the forest, silverbacks occasionally fight and try to recruit new females. But combat is relatively rare. Silverbacks prefer to discourage and intimidate opponents and predators with an elaborate series of chest-thumping roars, bluff charges, and other displays before resorting to fighting.

For most of the day, gorillas rest or forage for food. They will eat the leaves and shoots from 100 different plants, consuming an astounding total of 50 pounds of vegetation a day. In spite of the volume and variety in their diet, gorillas can be fussy eaters. Some peel each bamboo shoot and trim each leafy stalk of wild celery until it is just right. In the late morning they build crude day nests of flattened grass and leaves for their midday snoozes. At dusk, the dominant silverback begins to break branches to make a more elaborate night nest, and the others follow his example. Gorillas use a nest only once. Unlike chimps, gorillas spend very little time grooming each other. But they do frequently scratch, burp, and hiccup.

All gorillas are noticeable for their bulky, sway-backed frames, potbellies, thick arms, and squat legs. Their exposed skin is black and deeply lined. Their fur is black with undertones of rust, brown and blue. Mature males are called silverbacks because they develop a magnificent mantle of silver hair across the

Mountain gorillas rest in their day nest in Volcanos National Park in Rwanda. Mountain gorillas have thicker, shaggier fur to ward off the damp and cold at elevations above 10,000 feet.

A juvenile mountain gorilla isn't too heavy to reach the tender, new vegetation on top of shrubs.

torso and rump when they reach sexual maturity in their late teens. At the same time,

they lose chest hair, exposing rippling black pectorals. Their skulls develop a high, bony sagittal crest that forms an anchor for strong jaw muscles. On the back of the skull, the nuchal crest anchors thick neck muscles. Their incongruously tiny ears lie close to the head. Their eyes are small and amber brown.

Although gorillas have distinctive faces and expressions, it can be difficult to distinguish between individuals because they travel in groups and virtually melt into the forest. Every gorilla, however, has a unique nostril shape and pattern of wrinkles around the nose. To the trained eye, these subtle features, which are visible from a distance of several feet, can be a rapid method of identification. In the field, scientists sketch or photograph the noseprint of each gorilla in the group. The noseprints help them track individual apes over time and enable them to quickly spot new animals who have joined the group.

Gorillas are enormous. When they stand upright and stretch out—a position reserved for feeding or aggressive displays—they might be 6 feet 7 inches tall and might weigh more than 500 pounds. Most individuals tend to be smaller, however, especially in the wild where food supplies are not dependable and animals are more active.

Biologists recognize three subspecies of gorillas: the western lowland, the eastern lowland, and the mountain gorilla The western lowland gorilla, the most abundant, numbers between 9,000 to 40,000 and resides in the rain forests of Cameroon, Central African Republic, Equatorial Guinea, Gabon, and Congo.

Koundu's powerful muscles ripple as he knuckle-walks across the yard.

Distinguished by their broad faces and large skulls, western lowlands live in smaller social groups partly because their diets include ripe fruit (which is not plentiful), and because the animals must forage a large territory. The western lowland is the smallest subspecies, with males usually weighing 300 pounds and females weighing about 165 pounds. In captivity, western lowlands like Cenzoo and his family tend to grow considerably larger than their wild cousins.

The second subspecies, the eastern lowland, is native to isolated patches of rain forest in Zaire. Eastern lowlands are the tallest gorillas, often standing 5 feet 10 inches. They have the narrowest faces of the three subspecies and short black fur. Their population is estimated at 5,000 to 8,000.

The largest and most endangered of the three subspecies the mountain gorilla. About 620 individuals live high on the forested slopes of dominant

Grave marker of Digit, Dian Fossey's favorite gorilla. Digit was killed by poachers.

volcanoes that form the borders of Rwanda, Zaire and Uganda. Dian Fossey nicknamed them "gorillas in the mist" because their habitat at 9,000 to 12,000 feet is frequently shrouded in clouds. The trees in their homeland drip with lichen and moss, and temperatures dip to freezing at

night. Mature mountain males weigh 350 to 400 pounds; females weigh about 200 pounds. They have long hair, which sheds rain and provides insulation from the cold. Of the three subspecies, they have the most massive jaws.

Dian Fossey studied mountain gorillas for many years from Karisoke, the research facility she founded in Rwanda.

Most of what we know about gorilla breeding comes from landmark field studies of mountain gorillas by George Schaller and Dian Fossey in the 1960s and 1970s and from Fossey's successors in the 1980s. Zoo studies have provided increasing data about western lowlands gorillas since the 1970s as captive breeding programs expanded and

The sight of a gorilla mother with a youngster is a remarkable but, sadly, rare event.

improving technologies boosted their success rates. All of the subspecies breed infrequently—about once every four years. The low reproduction rate, combined with human encroachment on habitats, poaching, war, and other threats is a prescription for extinction.

The gestation period for gorillas is $8\frac{1}{2}$ months—2 weeks longer than chimps and orangutans but 2 weeks shorter than humans. Infants are born year-round; there is no specific breeding season. Gorilla mothers grow increasingly uncomfortable and lose some of their agility in the later months of pregnancy. Some have even been observed with swollen ankles. During the birth process, the mother lies down and swiftly delivers a single 4- to 6-pound baby. She bites through the umbilical cord and holds the infant to her chest so it can begin nursing. Unlike monkeys, newborn gorillas cannot immediately hold on to their mothers.

After a few days, the infant's pink skin darkens and begins to sprout thick fur. Gorilla infants develop twice as quickly as humans. Within 2 weeks they raise their heads. Their first teeth appear by 6 weeks. By 4 months they walk on all fours; by 6 months they are climbing. By 6 or 7 months, young gorillas taste and consume a variety of plants. Vegetation becomes a chief source of nutrition before the end of the first

year, and exploring for food is one way they demonstrate their independence. But a gorilla may nurse and climb on its mother's back for protection for 3 years or more. Gorillas do not suck their thumbs.

This young gorilla pops a mouthful. He will taste and consume a variety of plants.

Because gorillas are social animals, eventually every member of the group takes part in a young gorilla's upbringing. Mother gorillas will tolerate another female picking up her infant or shooing it away from danger. In some cases, lactating females have adopted the infants of others. After their arrival in

A view across Volcanos National Park. The park marks the border of Rwanda, Zaire, and Uganda and is home to the mountain gorillas.

Denver, for example, Bassa picked up Cenzoo and cuddled him before Jo-Ray-K did. Zookeepers also observed Cenzoo jumping on Bassa's considerable belly.

Bassa, the second adult female in the gorilla group. She sometimes watches Cenzoo for Jo-Ray-K.

In August 1996, visitors to Brookfield Zoo in suburban Chicago were witness to an unusual event involving a mother gorilla. A 3-year-old boy fell 18 feet into the gorilla pit. The toddler hit his head and was knocked unconscious. He also suffered a broken hand. Zookeepers used water hoses to keep the gorillas away from the boy before they attempted to rescue him. But an 8-year-old female western lowland gorilla named Binti Jua—which means daughter of sunshine in Swahili—ignored their commands and the water spray. She gently picked up the boy, cradled him in her arms and carried him to an access door to the exhibit. She retreated after depositing him on the ground. Zookeepers and paramedics entered the pen and removed the boy, who was rushed to the hospital.

Binti's tender treatment toward the injured boy generated worldwide interest. Television crews from around the world visited the zoo for weeks after. Animal behavior specialists stopped short of crediting the ape with anything more than good motherly instincts. Binti was carrying her own 16-month-old daughter when the accident occurred. George Insel, director of the Yerkes Primate Center of Emory University in Atlanta, said, "I really don't find it so surprising that a lactating female would pick up an injured infant from a related species."

Zoo officials, however, were careful to distinguish Binti's behavior from that of a wild gorilla. "She was responding to the type of training she has received," asserted Brookfield Zoo spokeswoman Melissa Pruett-Jones. "We have spent so much time with her to encourage and shape her maternal skills. That's the sort of thing she has been reinforced and rewarded for."

Although gruff silverbacks in the wild do not carry infants, they demonstrate tolerance as the youngsters play and tug for long periods. Females remain wary of their offspring getting too close to the silverbacks, however. As many as one-quarter of infant deaths involve dominant males.

At age 3, infant gorillas lose the tuft of white hair on their black rumps, which enabled their mothers to spot them in the dense green foliage of the forest floor. By that time, nursing also has slowed dramatically and the young have stopped riding on their mothers' backs. By 3 they are strong enough to walk long distances and forage for themselves, with occasional help and advice. In the wild, females, who become sexually mature at about age 8, leave their natal group and attach themselves to a new group. Males

become mature in their mid-teens and begin to develop the mantle of silvery fur.

Conflict within the social group occurs when a maturing male wants to breed with the females (even if he is not ready to lead

Koundu starts to thump his chest as Jo-Ray-K and Cenzoo play nearby.

Gorilla trackers help scientists locate gorilla groups in the forest and search trails for poachers' snares.

a group) and the reigning silverback is not ready to relinquish his position. After conflicts with the silverback, the male learns to subordinate himself and stay at the edge of the group, or he may leave to live alone in the forest or in a bachelor group until he can attract females and start a group of his own.

An adult gorilla's life is spent in a quiet routine of eating, breeding, and sleeping. They typically live about 35 years until they are weakened by parasites, food shortages, and disease. Infectious diseases, especially respiratory infections, can sweep through a gorilla group and quickly kill several members. Since the 1960s, poachers, trophy hunters, and war have taken their toll as well. But those losses are becoming less frequent as conservation treaties, national parks, and international media coverage combine to spotlight incidents and pressure nations to apprehend wildlife criminals.

The greatest threat to gorillas is humanity itself. As human populations in central Africa skyrocket, nations such as Rwanda, covering territories no larger than the state of Maryland, crowd as many as 9 million people within their contested borders. Villages and farms spread into what had been the gorillas' domain for millennia and people slash and burn the natural vegetation that the apes depend on for food and shelter. With loss of habitat, gorilla groups shrink as hunger and stress contribute to the premature deaths of adults and infants and the females' breeding cycles are interrupted. Soon they are gone.

Refugees in Rwanda await distribution of relief food from the United Nations. The refugees also use the gorillas' protected habitat illegally to snare small game and forage for food.

Chapter 4
The care and feeding of a gorilla family

Just before 8:00 A.M., zookeeper Bob Hamill unlocks the back door of Primate Panorama and slips into the darkened service corridor of the Great Ape House. The gorillas know he has arrived. They can smell and hear him. Koundu begins rummaging in his sleeping chamber and peers through his observation grating.

Early morning is Hamill's favorite time at work. In the summer, the sun is not yet blazing overhead. In the winter, the jungle heat simulated by the building's sophisticated climate control system feels comforting after the icy dash from the parking lot. And the crowds of visitors so eager to glimpse the Denver Zoo's gorilla troupe will not begin to press against the observation glass for at least another hour.

In the morning quiet, Hamill visits each of the four gorillas—Koundu, Jo-Ray-K with Cenzoo, and Bassa. Hamill moves slowly down the service corridor behind the sleeping chambers and greets each of them in low, measured tones. He spends a few minutes observing them as they relax in the night nests that they have fashioned out of straw. It looks very casual, but Hamill's every step and gesture is meaningful. He is reconnecting with the gorillas for another day, reinforcing the routine and building on the previous day's trust. Establishing bonds with such timid giants is a slow, tenuous process that began when the gorillas arrived in Denver from Chicago and it may take years to complete. Hamill is also conducting a quick appraisal. The gorillas and their home appear

Zookeeper Bob Hamill starts the morning of cleanup and maintenance.

unchanged and nothing unusual appears to have occurred overnight. In particular, Hamill closely observes changes in Cenzoo's behavior and demeanor. As an infant, Cenzoo spent most of the early hours nursing drowsily, nestled in his mother's coarse fur. As Cenzoo matures, Hamill frequently finds him playing in the chamber he shares with his mother or peeking out of the grating and down the service corridor.

Cenzoo spends a lot of time snuggling up to his protective mother.

It will not be easy for Hamill to establish a relationship with the young ape. For the first few years, Cenzoo will stay close to his mother, and she is likely to whisk him up into the canopy netting of the playroom or into a corner of the sleeping chamber if she feels the scrutiny of humans is too intense. By the time Cenzoo is a strapping, rambunctious adolescent, the zookeeper hopes to be on friendly terms with him.

Despite Hamill's care, things do not always go according to plan. One fall morning, Hamill related, Cenzoo was sitting alone near the hallway grating of the sleeping chamber. Hamill walked down the service corridor as usual, but apparently Cenzoo did not notice him in his brown zoo uniform until he was right by the door. "He screamed and hollered," Hamill said. "I must've really scared him."

Hamill has been a keeper for the zoo's great apes since 1979. He cares for the gorillas five days a week. On his days off, his duties are assumed by zookeeper Jody Hodges, who has worked with the Denver Zoo's primates since 1979. When she is not with the gorillas, Hodges assists with the orangutans who live next door. Both Hamill and Hodges majored in biology in college and planned on zoo careers. But neither set their sights on working with great apes, although apes are among the most popular animals on any zoo's roster and among the most challenging animals to care for in captivity.

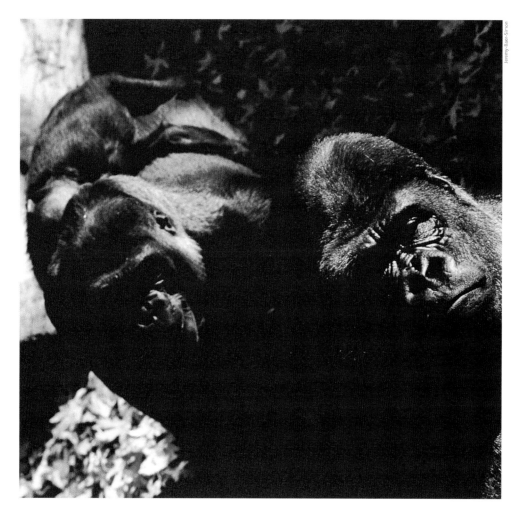

The whole family takes a stroll. It's a lot of work for zoo keepers to care for the gorillas seven days a week.

Reliability is an important characteristic in caring for gorillas. So is unflappability. Although gorillas are the largest and strongest primates, they are surprisingly timid. It usually takes a long time for them to become accustomed to new zookeepers and new surroundings. Zookeepers try to maintain a familiar routine because changes will easily unsettle the gorillas. When Cenzoo and his family arrived from Chicago, his previous zookeeper, Eric Meyer, stayed for several days to teach members of the Denver Zoo staff how to handle the group and to slowly introduce each of the gorillas to them. "We started from scratch together," Hodges said 8 months after the gorillas' arrival. "We're still getting used to each other."

Part of getting to know the new gorilla family was discovering their fondness for cantaloupe.

Koundu interacts with zookeepers several times a day through the metal gratings of his sleeping chamber. The shyer females often behave more subtly. They generally devote their attentions to Cenzoo. They prefer to remain in the distance, sometimes three stories high at the top of the playroom climbing structure. Hamill and Hodges have no direct access to Cenzoo. "Most people ask us if we go into the enclosure with them—the answer is no," Hamill said. "Koundu can be quite grabby if you get too close to the door grating. He's quite fast and you have to be wary of him."

When the early morning check is completed, Hamill goes back into the apes' "kitchen" to prepare their food for the day. In the wild, an adult gorilla might eat 50 pounds of nettles, wild celery, and fruit in a day. In the zoo, the gorillas' diet is a nutritionally balanced commercial biscuit made of grains and vegetables. The menu is supplemented by green vegetables and fruits. For treats, Hamill will offer small measures of peanuts, peanut butter, raisins, grapes, bananas, and, depending on the season, peaches, plums,

Left: Zookeeper
Bob Hamill carefully
measures out dry in-
gredients for the go-
rillas' daily porridge.

Right: Gorillas
don't eat bananas
in the wild, but they
enjoy them in a
zoo setting.

and melons. The fruit treats are not unnatural for western lowland gorillas, in particular. Unlike mountain gorillas, who live at very high elevations, western lowlands consume fruits that grow in their warm forests.

Every morning, Hamill prepares a porridge that is based on a recipe provided by Eric Meyer of the Lincoln Park Zoo in Chicago. He crumbles biscuits in a bowl and adds warm water, cooked rice, and baby cereal. At first, he tried to serve the porridge in "bowls" made of paper toweling. But he soon discovered the gorillas were eating their paper bowls, too. Now he fashions the bowls from lettuce leaves. The porridge represents another effort to keep the gorillas' routine as familiar as possible. But it has another purpose. "It's an easy way to give them medications," Hamill said.

As a rule, zookeepers do not routinely feed gorilla infants such as Cenzoo until they about 3 years old. Cenzoo will rely on mother's milk for nourishment. Zookeepers did notice Cenzoo sampling the adults' biscuits and vegetables when he was about 5 months old, but he was only acting out of curiosity. "He puts things in his mouth like a human baby," Hamill said.

In the wild, gorillas spend several hours a day foraging for celery, bamboo, and other plants. Depending on the forest density, food availability, terrain, weather, and other factors, a gorilla group might browse all day through a territory of several square miles. It is impossible to duplicate such an environment or provide foraging opportunities in an urban zoo setting. But modern zookeepers find it unacceptable to feed gorillas by the old "prison method" of dumping food on the floor or in a tub. To encourage the gorillas to use their foraging instincts and to feed in a more natural way, Hamill and Hodges hide the food in the thick straw bedding throughout the exhibit. This approach makes eating a challenging activity that more closely resembles life in the wild.

The zookeepers also take advantage of mealtime to perform routine cleaning and

Zookeeper Bob Hamill tries to select different spots where he puts
food to encourage gorillas to use their foraging instincts.

Wild gorillas can eat up to 50 pounds of vegetation per day. In the zoo, commercial biscuits provide their essential nutrition. Vegetables and fruits hidden around their habitat offer variety and encourage foraging.

Jeremy Baer-Simon

Zookeeper Bob Hamill rakes the indoor play area while the gorillas are outside.

Cenzoo: The story of a baby gorilla

maintenance. When the gorillas are in their large indoor playroom, Hamill places food in their sleeping chambers or in a secure area known as the holding room. The aroma of the food—and, increasingly, the sight and sounds of a zookeeper working—lures them into these areas. They are contained there while Hamill washes the playroom floor and changes the straw bedding. Then he puts food in the playroom so he can clean the sleeping chambers and the holding room. In warm weather, Hamill opens the outside door and gives the gorillas access to their one-acre exercise yard. This simple strategy works most of the time. But on some days the gorillas do not cooperate and it can take much of the morning to complete routine chores.

By 4:30 P.M., the crowd of visitors begins to thin. The zookeepers have long since completed their routine chores. They record their observations about the gorillas' habits and health in a daily log, including what they ate, the medications they might have received,

and the appearance of their stools. Hamill adds a description of any unusual behaviors that the gorillas might have displayed, such as Cenzoo pulling himself up to the playroom's raised platforms without his mother's assistance, or Koundu becoming exceptionally agitated by zoo visitors.

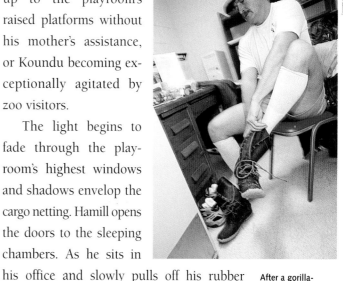

The light begins to fade through the playroom's highest windows and shadows envelop the cargo netting. Hamill opens the doors to the sleeping chambers. As he sits in his office and slowly pulls off his rubber overboots, the gorillas move inside the secluded rooms and begin to assemble their night nests from straw and strips of paper. Another day ends at Primate Panorama. Tomorrow morning, they will do it again.

After a gorilla-sized workout, Zookeeper Bob Hamill removes his overboots and takes a much deserved rest.

Chapter 5
Cenzoo: Growing and exploring

Jo-Ray-K spied a tasty biscuit hidden in a great mound of straw bedding. In one motion, she shrugged baby Cenzoo from her back and snatched up the tiny treasure with her huge, hairy hand. Cenzoo sat bewildered as his mother retreated to the corner of the playroom. Jo-Ray-K turned her back on her 5-month-old infant and the rest of her gorilla family and began to gnaw contentedly. Gorillas in the wild rarely put down their infants; left unattended, the young would be an easy meal for a predator. By comparison, the captive-born Jo-Ray-K appeared to be rather indifferent and easily distracted.

For a moment, the coal-black infant looked tiny and forlorn, his head poking out of the yellow straw not much higher than the biscuit that his mother found. But then he gathered himself up on his spindly limbs and began to stagger-walk and crawl resolutely toward her. In the wild, baby gorillas do not walk until they are 7 to 10 months old and zookeeper Bob Hamill noted Cenzoo's behavior. "I think Jo-Ray-K is forcing him to be more independent. When he was 3 months old, he was doing things that a 7-month-old gorilla in the wild would do," he said. "I've seen him get up and walk from one end of the indoor habitat to the other in order to be with her. It takes him about five minutes with a rest stop halfway, but he gets it done."

Cenzoo moves about the play area while following his mother closely.

Cenzoo shows little fear on the high platform.

On this occasion, Cenzoo's journey took him within a few feet of his hulking father, Koundu. As Cenzoo disappeared into his father's car-sized shadow, Koundu coiled his rippling muscles for what might become a chest-thumping, window-pounding, straw-trampling display of supreme maleness. He showed no sign that he knew or cared that his son was in harm's way.

Jo-Ray-K and Cenzoo rest in the upstairs rigging.

But Koundu's movement, for all of its power, turned out to be the prelude to a stretch and a yawn. Then he relaxed. A few seconds later, Cenzoo emerged unscathed in the daylight. Moments like these remind Hamill and other zookeepers of their inability to control events or intervene when things appear to be going awry.

Koundu has calmed down considerably since moving from Chicago to Denver. At Lincoln Zoo in Chicago, officials were con-cerned because he was often surly and agitated. The crowds of visitors were never ending and the cramped, old exhibit housed other silverbacks that may have threatened his status. In Denver, his surroundings are more spacious, and the nearest silverback is 65 miles south at the zoo in Colorado Springs. When Koundu's male outbursts and demonstrations occur, Jo-Ray-K grabs Cenzoo and heads for the highest cargo net in the playroom. Bassa, hot on her heels, also heads up the rope rigging. "I just hold my breath a lot of the time," Hamill said. "Koundu could be rough on Cenzoo, or Cenzoo might just get in the way. And there's not a thing I can do about it."

Sometimes Cenzoo gets himself into trouble. And zookeepers cannot control that, either: It is all part of growing up. At 8 months old, Cenzoo (who weighed nearly twice as much as the day he arrived) still had spindly legs. But his arms had grown longer and had become more muscular. Standing on

Sometimes a rope is as good as a jungle vine.

the playroom floor, he could use his powerful little hands and thickening shoulders to hoist himself up the 3-foot ledge to a raised platform. He had become large and strong enough to grip the smaller ropes in the climbing structure and the netting. "One day I looked up and I saw Cenzoo hanging from the top of the climbing structure by one hand," Hamill said. "I just held my breath. But he was fine."

Cenzoo becomes more curious everyday and often investigates anything that one of the adult gorillas discards. Even familiar items like straw bedding suddenly became fascinating to him. From his side of the observation glass, he watches the visitors as in-

Jo-Ray-K steadies the rope as Cenzoo plays.

Cenzoo always makes a spectacle of himself as he and Jo-Ray-K parade for visitors behind the glass windows of the indoor play area.

tently as they watch him. Sometimes he even plays to the crowd a bit. "One morning he was sitting on his mother's back as she walked the length of the observation window. He stuck out his hand and dragged his palm along the glass as if was waving to them. He was definitely responding to them," Hamill said. Although Cenzoo stays close to his mother, he no longer clings continuously to her fur. He hitches a ride on her hind leg, often standing on top of her large foot as she walks. Or he scampers up to her thick neck and raises his head for a better view.

Jo-Ray-K usually tolerates Cenzoo's antics. But when she wants to get someplace quickly—for example, if she is weary of being observed by zoo visitors and yearns for privacy—she will hoist Cenzoo onto her broad back and clamber up the thick supports of the climbing structure, all in one motion. Usually, she is headed for the uppermost cargo netting. Once the two of them are safely three stories overhead, Cenzoo will dismount and begin exploring again—without a net below him.

In a few years, Cenzoo will interact and learn more from Koundu. But a silverback's primary job in the wild is to protect his group from outside threats; unfortunately there is not much work or territory for a silverback in a limited zoo setting. He can forage for food that Hamill might have hidden, but he cannot scour a large area of forest for the place that the group will feed and spend the night.

If Cenzoo were housed in a traditional zoo featuring old-fashioned cages or tile rooms, he would have even fewer opportunities to explore and experiment. Although it might be easier on Hamill's nerves, both zoo curators and critics endorse the current trend in the United States and other industrialized nations of building habitat-style zoo

An attentive Koundu protects his group in the indoor play area.

enclosures. The new facilities feature the latest in climate controls, air filtering, sanitation, noise buffering, and fire prevention. Every seam and joint is welded for extra strength and the public observation windows are nearly 2 inches thick to absorb a gorilla's pounding. Despite the technology and security, the more spacious and open architecture of the habitats allows the animals to live in social groups and behave more naturally. The new exhibits are more interesting for the animals, and the visitors, too. The $14-million, 7.5-acre Primate Panorama, which opened to visitors in summer 1996, is one of the biggest and most elaborate of modern, habitat-style exhibits, especially among inner-city zoos.

The gorilla family enjoys climbing around on the indoor climbing structure.

During cold weather, the gorillas are largely limited to their indoor playroom, their sleeping chambers, and the holding area. But in warm weather, their world is twice as large. Beyond the service door at the far end of the holding room is an acre of open yard dotted with leafy trees. Thick tree trunks lie scattered in the tall grass. Extending several feet from the playroom door is a soft carpet of wood chips. Along the walls of the yard, a canopy protects the gorillas on rainy days. The underside of the canopy has been fitted with space heaters to radiate heat in the spring and autumn when skies might be clear, but the temperature is crisper than in the equatorial forests in the gorillas' native Africa. Although the yard is not as large as a gorilla's natural territory, it is much more spacious and stimulating than the slick-tiled boxes in older zoos.

Cenzoo and his family were at Primate Panorama for several weeks before they were introduced to the outside yard. The zookeepers wanted to be certain that the gorillas felt safe and comfortable in their new surroundings before the door to a larger and different

Visitors get close to Koundu in his indoor play area. Some visitors may find Koundu's size and appearance overwhelming.

Koundu's first outdoor experience in Denver was to feel the warm sun on his face and torso.

world was opened. Although Koundu and the females had access to a small yard in Chicago, Cenzoo's only outdoor experience was his brief press conference on the tarmac at the Denver airport when he arrived. It was a warm June morning several weeks before the exhibit's public opening. Hamill simply opened the door to the yard and retreated into the service corridor. Sunlight and fresh air streamed into the climate-controlled exhibit. When the gorillas were let out of their sleeping chambers, they immediately noticed the change. Keeping Cenzoo and the females behind him, Koundu knuckle-walked determinedly to the open door.

Hamill had raced to the roof of the exhibit for an overall view of the yard. The event was off-limits to the public, but zoo employees—from curators to gardeners—crowded around the fences to watch. For nearly 30 minutes, Koundu remained just inside of the threshold. Occasionally he would lean out into the sunlight, look suspiciously from side to side, and then snatch a wood chip with his large, thick fingers. He would peer at it and taste it. Several minutes passed before he gingerly swung one of his massive haunches onto the soft carpet of chips. Then he moved his other haunch, so that he was sitting just outside of the door instead of inside it. A few times he stood on

Koundu gradually became more comfortable with the outdoor environment. Initially, he only ventured a few steps at a time.

his hind legs, stretching to his full height of 5 feet 4 inches. He stroked the rough surface of the simulated rock walls of the building. The audience encouraged him to advance into the yard. Zoo curators leaned against the fence and called his name, "Koundu, c'mon Koundu." But he would not budge. Then Hamill tried. But when Koundu realized that someone—or something—was on the roof, he became even more nervous. Hamill's presence above and behind him was threatening and he retreated to the safety of the threshold.

Koundu continued his pattern of advancing and retreating for most of the morning. As noon approached, the female gorillas' curiosity overcame his admonitions to stay back. They squeezed past his bulk in the doorway and emerged into the sunny yard. First came Jo-Ray-K with Cenzoo clinging to her back. She kept her eyes fixed on the wood chips and paused to examine them in much the same way Koundu had done. Cenzoo kept his bald head pressed against her shoulder blade, but his eyes were opened wide as he stared at the grass, trees, and the crowd of people beyond the fence. Never before had he seen an open space with tall trees. Then Bassa ambled up alongside them. With Koundu still peering up warily at the roof where Hamill's voice had come from, the other gorillas slowly moved off the wood chip carpet and onto the grass, investigating, sniffing and tasting.

Jo-Ray-K adventured into the outdoor area with Cenzoo clinging to her back.

The gorillas' timid behavior is in marked contrast to the 28 other species of great apes and lesser monkeys in Primate Panorama. Captive orangutans, for example—unlike gorillas—are curious about foreign objects and they adapt quickly to new surroundings. They continually climb up and down ropes in their exhibit and play with a variety of boxes, T-shirts and other safe "toys" that have been made available to them. When the door to the yard was first opened for the Denver orangutans, they explored the far side of their outside yard within a few minutes.

Gorillas are much more creatures of habit than orangutans. Their concentration on the familiar contributes to making life in the group peaceful and relaxed. On that first day in their yard, the females used the closest fallen tree trunk as a boundary. Every day they would venture a little farther out. The pattern continued through the gorillas' first summer at the zoo. As Koundu sat with his arms crossed, the females and Cenzoo would venture into the

tall grass 30 or 40 feet from the door. In contrast, Koundu remained much further back from the fence and the observation areas where the public gathers. Although the yard is very enriching, Hamill realizes it might take Koundu another summer or longer to move beyond the familiarity of the wood chips. "Once I even sprinkled peanuts on the far side of that first log," he said. "He stayed on the wood chips and stretched out as far as he could in order to get one. But he never would walk into the grass to get one."

As the months pass and Cenzoo grows larger, he starts to sample the outdoor environment. Instead of riding on his mother's back high off the ground, he hitches a ride on her hind leg, reaching out for grass and sticks as she walks. When she stops, he dismounts and sit next to her, occupying himself with a twig or a stem. "He's the most curious of the gorillas," Hamill said. "As he gets older, he might be the first one to go all the way to the other side of the yard."

Cenzoo learns that autumn leaves don't taste nearly as good as the green leaves and vegetables.

Chapter 6
Cenzoo and Pablo: Two gorillas with different futures

Visitors giggle at Cenzoo's antics as he frolics in his playroom. Every day many ask zookeepers, "Can you get in there with him?"

Not a very good idea. Despite their timid personalities, regular exposure to humans behind glass barriers and dependence on zookeepers for food, the gorillas in Primate Panorama are not habituated to humans. Gorillas like to keep distance and clear lines of sight between intruders and their young, at least until they are reassured there is no threat. Without a hill or a ravine to give them an advantage, Koundu and the females would feel threatened by a human intrusion and would likely protect Cenzoo at all costs.

In 1993, on a reporting trip to Volcanoes National Park, I learned first-hand of a gorilla's response to human intruders. I had accompanied a pair of scientists with the Dian Fossey Gorilla Fund who were trying to determine whether months of civil war had disrupted the animals' peaceful existence and reversed the rare species' slow population gains since poaching had been curtailed in the 1980s.

After 3 hours of hiking up steep, muddy trails, we arrived at Dian Fossey's research camp, Karisoke, which the Fossey Fund had maintained and enlarged following her murder in 1985. As Rwanda's civil war had flared, however, researchers had to be evacuated repeatedly. We found the unprotected camp

Cenzoo will grow up in an environment that is different in many ways from his relatives in the wild. One difference is his relative safety from the type of human intrusions that are destroying the gorilla's native habitats.

View of Karisoke Research Center (1993) upon entering camp.This remote gorilla research camp high in the mountain of Rwanda was founded by Dian Fossey and was destroyed in a civil war in 1995.

pillaged by rebels and poachers; but there were no alternatives, so we stayed in the ruins for several days. Periodically we would venture out of camp to find and count the mountain gorillas in several social groups. One day our mission was to locate Group 5, which had 36 gorillas and was considered to be the largest gorilla group on record. We hiked to the deeply forested saddle between two dormant volcanoes in the park's southwestern zone and trailed the group until midday. At that point the gorillas paused to eat lunch and to nap in a ravine above 10,000 feet and we were able to catch up with them.

Dieter Stecklis negotiates with villagers to carry scientific gear up the mountain trail to Karisoke.

Although the researchers had been monitoring Group 5 for 3 years and the group had been studied for 2 decades, we approached cautiously. The researchers had been absent for several months, and without protection from park rangers the gorillas might have been frightened by soldiers or poachers during the recent upheaval. But the gorillas scarcely looked up as we arrived. Our mood soon turned grim. The group's dominant silverback, Ziz, should have come down to check us out. Estimated to weigh 500 pounds (less than Koundu), Ziz was a colossus by wild gorilla standards, but he was more than just big and strong. He had a regal bearing and primatologists had long admired his leadership in keeping such a large group together while the park was being destroyed by war and a booming human population. We sadly concluded that Ziz was dead, an assumption that was confirmed later by the discovery of what was believed to be his skeleton. Unlike many gorillas that have been shot in recent years, Ziz probably died from parasites or as a result of combat with competing males.

Nevertheless, we still had to count the remaining gorillas in Group 5 and determine which younger silverback might be trying to

Cenzoo and Pablo: Two gorillas with different futures   67

replace Ziz as its leader. We crept up the hillside, mimicking the gorillas' grunting sounds and pretending to chew on vegetation to put them at ease. Despite the poor footing on the steep slope, we knew it was important not to stand up because the sight might frighten them. And we knew that when we encountered the males competing to replace Ziz that we should not stare directly into their eyes. A silverback interprets a stare as a challenge to his status as leader and he will prepare to fight.

A mountain gorilla endures another cloudburst in Volcanos National Park. Despite the frequent storms in their habitat, mountain gorillas do not like the rain and seek cover until a storm passes.

The gorillas were scattered across the hillside, and we split up in order to see all of them. Many of the females allowed us to approach within a few feet. They appeared healthy, although a few bore fresh wounds that might have been the results of rough mating or fights with another gorilla group. Several females were nursing infants as young as Cenzoo; some were trying to keep tabs on youngsters that were a few years older and more adventurous.

Our assumption that Ziz was dead was supported by the sight of three younger silverbacks trying to assume control of the whole group or parts of it. They took up prominent positions in the ravine and each female would choose one of the males and circle him as they picked through the undergrowth for tasty leaves. In was by this quiet behavior that the females eventually would decide which of the males offered the best protection and breeding prospects.

Pablo, one of the competing males, had been sizing me up for about 30 minutes. He was well known to the researchers. Fossey, who had seen him as a youngster, noted that he was mischievous. Now he was about 18 years old and observers reported that he had become ornery and unpredictable as he matured sexually and began vying for females. "Be careful not to get too close to Pablo," the

Pablo, an 18-year-old mountain gorilla silverback
new to his role as group leader, glares at me as I mistakenly
get too close to a female and her infant.

scientists warned me. "And don't get between him and a female, especially if she has an infant." I tried to keep an eye out for him. Given his girth and menacing stare, how hard could this be? Very, as he repeatedly demonstrated. He popped out of a dense thicket of shrubs on my left as I was trying to photograph an older female named Maggie and her baby. I retreated and moved downhill. Later, as I was traversing the hillside for more photos, I noticed that he was above me, shadowing my every step. But he seemed to be ignoring me and appeared more interested in foraging.

A little gorilla about 3 years old was frolicking on its back next to its mother. I crept closer for a better photo, but the vines and shrubs obscured my view. Straining for a better angle, I forgot my instructions and leaned toward the youngster with my camera raised. Suddenly Pablo reappeared just 10 yards away, directly in front of me; he rose silently above the vegetation, glaring. It was the same stare that Koundu gives a zoo visitor who lingers in front of his enclosure.

I froze in my awkward pose. Then Pablo raised his huge fists to beat his chest. Silverbacks have a repertoire of gestures and vocalizations designed to warn foes. Chest-thumping, one of the most familiar, is meant to demonstrate the silverback's size and power. I expected to hear a hollow thumping like a bass drum. Instead, a sharp crack whizzed past my head like a rifle shot. For good measure, he fired off a drumroll of consecutive beats that blasted my ears and ricocheted around the ravine.

I lost my balance and hit the thorny vegetation with a splat. I looked up and saw Pablo was still there. The scientific record is filled with reports of researchers who have been bruised and battered by bluffing gorillas. In the most serious altercations, a few have been bitten, but no one has been killed. Although I knew that I should not run because Pablo would chase me, I found it hard

As I stepped backward, I lost my balance and tumbled down the hillside.

to remember my instructions when he was close enough to smell. He made another gesture in my direction. I twisted away from

A close look at native vegetation awaited me at the bottom of the hill. My fall was stopped by a shrub.

him and rose to flee. Or I tried to. One half-step and I tumbled and rolled down the hillside through red mud and green gorilla dung. I stopped when a shrub ensnared me.

I survived that encounter. But the events of that day and what I saw on that trip convinced me of the threat to the gorillas' survival. Sadly, decades of field studies, conservation programs ,and public education have only managed to stabilize their populations in some areas after years of swift decline. Gorillas, who have no natural enemies except for humans, have been prized for trophies for 2,500 years. Through the 1970s, poachers hunted them down to capture the infants for sale on the black market. They collected gorilla hands,

feet, and skulls for ashtrays and other souvenirs. In some remote villages in central African nations, you might still find gorilla meat in the market or served in restaurants. Although international conservation treaties, successful captive breeding programs, and the financial incentives of tourism have largely eliminated the lucrative gorilla trade, their numbers in the wild still dwindle. At the core of the problem is human overpopulation. The population growth rate in many central African nations is more than 3 percent annually. As cities and villages expand, the need for food and building materials increases. The tropical forests where gorillas live are being felled for their timber and burned for cattle pastures, plantations, and farms. Even in national parks where the gorillas are legally protected, their habitats are being eroded.

Nowhere is this situation more apparent than in the cramped rugged corner where the borders of Zaire, Uganda, and Rwanda

Rwandan coffee and tea plantations encroach on native mountain gorilla habitat.

converge, and where the world's only mountain gorillas live. Their protected park was one of the first to be established in Africa in 1922, but since then, small-plot subsistence farms and larger-scale government agricultural experiments have been steadily pressing against its borders and redrawing them in some places. The park straddling the Virunga mountain range is only a few miles wide. From the gorillas' range high on the forested slopes of dormant volcanoes, they can easily see freshly plowed red hillsides. Where recently there was lush green forest, a patchwork of coffee and tea plantations and farm plots for potatoes, cassava, and bananas spreads.

Since 1994, ethnic warfare and genocide in Rwanda and Zaire have compounded the problem. The world's 620 remaining mountain gorillas are trapped in their tiny habitat—a buffer zone in the conflict. Desperate refugees use the park as a supermarket for food, firewood, and shelter as international humanitarian workers are prevented by rogue militias from distributing relief supplies.

Mountain Gorillas live in an uncertain world
complicated by war and human suffering, as well
as their own limited habitat and genetic isolation.

Refugees line up early in the day for food distribution. A population explosion and villagers fleeing civil war continue to deplete food and habitat for native gorillas.

Anti-poaching patrols and scientists have tried to continue operating amid the chaos, but their efforts have been underfunded and sporadic since 1994. Conservationists who attempt to protect eastern and western lowland gorillas elsewhere in central Africa may not be hobbled by war and refugees, but they feel the twin pressures of human overpopulation and habitat loss just as acutely. And without the horrors of war to draw the world's attention, their programs often receive even less support than those that benefit the mountain gorillas.

Saving gorillas in the wild in the twenty-first century will require more than just the establishment of more parks, ranger patrols, and anti-poaching sweeps to cut down snares from the gorillas' paths. Political stability, economic prosperity, and serious efforts to curb human population growth must be pursued regardless of the religious importance and cultural prestige that some people place on families with 10, 12, and even 15 children. More efficient methods must be developed to help farmers grow crop surpluses on existing plots, and light manufacturing must be introduced to establish a consumer economy to relieve the pressure on the land. Rules to protect the gorillas' sanctuary must be strictly enforced, and efforts to protect and study the gorillas' health and fertility must be enlarged.

Otherwise, the next century, perhaps the next few decades, will be the last for gorillas in the wild. Gorillas in captivity, like Cenzoo, will soon be all that remains of the world's largest primate.

Without peace and improved protection, conservationists doubt they will survive long into the twenty-first century.

Cenzoo and his family have found a
new, safe home at the Denver Zoo.

80   Cenzoo: The story of a baby gorilla

Recommended Reading

Diamond, Jared. *The Third Chimpanzee: The Evolution and Future of the Human Animal.* New York: Harper Collins, 1992.

Fossey, Dian. *Gorillas in the Mist.* Boston: Houghton Mifflin, 1983.

Grizimek, Bernhard, ed. *Grizimek's Animal Encyclopedia, Volume 10: Mammals.* New York: Van Nostrand, 1972.

MacDonald, David, ed. *The Encyclopedia of Mammals.* New York: Facts on File Publications, 1985.

National Audubon Society. *Field Guide to African Wildlife.* New York: Knopf, 1995.

Redmond, Ian. *Eyewitness Books: Gorilla.* New York: Knopf, 1995.

Schaller, George, with photographs by Mike Nichol. *Gorilla—Struggle for Survival in the Virungas.* New York: Farrar, Straus and Giroux, 1989.

Recommended Viewing

Bell, George Jr., *Twilight of the Gorilla.* Mutual of Omaha Spirit of Adventure Series, 1991. Videocassette.